How to Pick Vintage Motorcycles

Frank Fritz

How to Pick Vintage
Motorcycles

Frank Fritz

www.whitman.com

How to Pick Vintage Motorcycles

www.whitman.com

© 2014 Whitman Publishing, LLC

3101 Clairmont Rd. • Suite G • Atlanta, GA 30329

This book is not associated with nor endorsed by The History Channel® or American Pickers®.

Correspondence concerning this book may be directed to the publisher, Attn: How to Pick Vintage Motorcycles, at the address above.

Photography by Amy Richmond: www.amyrichmondphotography.com.

ISBN: 0794840698

Printed in the United States

Scan this QR code to browse Whitman Publishing's full catalog of books.

Table of Contents

I had heard a lot of good things about Victory's new entry-level bike, the Eight Ball, so I bought this one brand new when I went out to Sturgis in 2013.

How I Became A Picker

I'm Frank Fritz, and I'm an American picker.

You may have seen me tooling around the countryside on the "American Pickers" television show on the History Channel looking for collectibles in old barns, garages and warehouses. The idea is to find something someone doesn't want or need any more, pay a fair price for it and then resell it on my website. It's a fun and interesting way to make a living.

It's also something I've been doing for a long time, beginning when I was a little kid growing up in Iowa, where I still live to this day. But there was a bigger goal in those early years.

I wanted things, a lot of things, but most of all I wanted a bike — a motorcycle.

My mom told me that was fine, but if I wanted things, I had to earn them myself. So, I shoveled snow in the winter and mowed lawns in the summer. I had maybe 15 to 17 walks to shovel, and I could make $200 to $300 every big snow. In the summer, I didn't have that many lawns to mow, but that was a little steadier. I also got a job when I was 12 at the Quad Cities Automatic Sprinkler Company. I would empty wastebaskets and vacuum the carpets. I wasn't old enough to work legally — I had to wait until I was 14 — but they would slip me a little money under the table. So I made some money, and started to accumulate things.

■ (Preceding page) One of the first motorcycles I bought as a kid was a Suzuki RM 125 in 1978. I rode it on trails near the Mississippi River and on a mountain called "The Lyme Pits." (Below) A closeup of the cylinder and carburetor on the RM 125, which I paid for by shoveling snow and mowing lawns.

Since I was still so young, I had to start out with a motorbike — you know, one of those things with a lawn mower engine. But that got old after a while and I wanted something bigger. Well, just down the street from my house was a guy named George T. Bennett, and he was a motorcycle mechanic instructor. I was good friends with his son — we still hang out some — and we started riding some of the bikes his dad had. He must have had 50 or 60 of them. We'd take them out to an old lime pit near where I worked and we'd run the bikes around the pit.

It was about that time, though, that dirt bikes became pretty cool, so we started buying those. I had a PS 125, a PS 159, an RM 125 and a few other bikes we'd ride, and we'd take those out all the time.

▪ (Preceding page, left) A closeup of the motor on my new Victory bike. (Below) The Eight Ball has quickly become my favorite bike to ride.

■ (Below) This is my 1962 Harley-Davidson Hard Tail chopper. These bikes were very popular in the 1970s. This is a custom bike featuring a springer front end and a hard tail frame. There aren't any shocks on these bikes, so you feel a stronger impact. (Opposite page) The Harley Hard Tail is powered by a 900cc Sportster motor.

■ (Left) This photo of the H-D Hard Tail chopper provides a better view of the springer front end. (Above and opposite page) I bought this Honda CRF 150 slightly used for $900. It was built in 2002 or 2003, and it is an all-purpose motorcycle for riding trails.

The problem was, I still wasn't old enough to ride on the street legally. So, my mom told me we had to walk them down the alley and across a busy street before we could fire them up. Pushing the bikes up and down the alley and across the street lasted, oh, maybe a week before we were starting them up and riding down the alley and in the street. The police knew us, of course. Bettendorf was a small town, and they'd stop us once in a while and tell us we couldn't ride on the side-walk or in the street. And then sometimes they'd show up at the front door and tell my mom and dad what we'd been doing. We'd get in trouble for a while, but then we'd be right back riding the dirt bikes.

Falling In Love With Harleys

After a while, I sort of lost interest in the dirt bikes, even though I still have a few of them. The main thing was I wanted to ride on the streets. I wanted a big bike, a Harley-Davidson.

I guess that came from when we lived in California for a short time. My stepdad would come home from work on his big Harley, and once in a while he would let me ride it around the block. That was when motorcycles first got in my blood. The only stipulation was we couldn't let my mom know, because she would have absolutely flipped out.

Then, when I was 15, my stepdad helped me get my own bike, a 1964 Harley, and it went on from there. I still wasn't able to ride it on the streets, though. You couldn't get a license until you were 16 in Iowa. So, I still had to wait until I could — legally — ride the streets.

All of this may sound like it was all work, some play and not a lot of school, but I worked that in, too. It may sound like I didn't like school, but that wasn't the case. I loved school. I just did it a little different.

■ (Preceding page and left) The CRF 150 has a 4-stroke and can be putted around at speeds of 20 to 30 mph. It's mostly used for fun!

■ HOW I BECAME A PICKER

My freshman, sophomore and junior years, I went to summer school every year. That meant I could get out every day all year before noon and go to work. That didn't mean I didn't know anyone at school or not hang out with anyone. In fact, I pretty much knew everybody and got along with about everybody — the jocks, the greasers, the little fat kids no one would talk to. I just loved school. Even though I loved to learn and was pretty much a sponge when it came to school, I probably wasn't as good a student as I could have been. I was maybe a B student for the four years, but when I graduated, I had 38 credits and you only needed 32 to graduate. More than that, when I got out of Bettendorf High, there were probably only 30 kids out of the 700 in my class that I didn't know. I am proud of that.

However, I wasn't going to go to college, and I knew that. My parents couldn't afford to send me to Iowa City to be a Hawkeye, and I really didn't want to go. I was working at the sprinkler company, and I saw those sprinkler fitters making 20 bucks an hour, which looked pretty good to me.

■ (Below and opposite page) I've had this 1989 Harley Heritage Soft Tail for a long time. The paint is called Root Beer and Cream, and they only made 5,000 of them. In 30-some years, I've only seen one of these bikes at Sturgis.

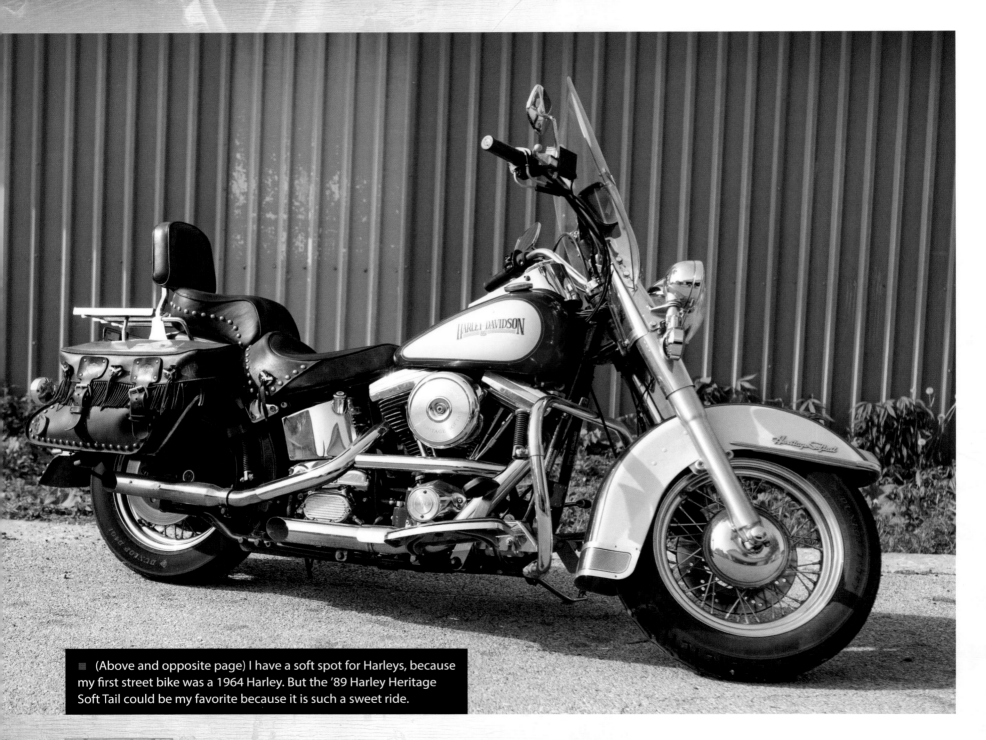

■ (Above and opposite page) I have a soft spot for Harleys, because my first street bike was a 1964 Harley. But the '89 Harley Heritage Soft Tail could be my favorite because it is such a sweet ride.

■ HOW I BECAME A PICKER

By the time I was 16 and legal to drive on the streets, and between the sprinkler company and weekends at Coast-to-Coast Hardware, I was putting away money. I still wanted things like motorcycles, guns and fishing poles. It was a bit funny, though. We lived in a pretty nice neighborhood, but my parents didn't have the kind of money most of the rest of families did. But, I had more money than the rest of kids because I was always hustling and working.

■ (Below and opposite page) This is my 1942 Harley-Davidson Flathead that I bought in 2005. I had it restored, and it has a few reproduction parts. I spent $9,000 on this bike and now it is worth close to $20,000. It's referred to as a "45," which is the maximum speed it can go.

00021

00022

Working For Bike Money

You may wonder how a kid from a town in Iowa could afford something like that. After all, the popular conception of life in Iowa is a bunch of small towns scattered among the cornfields and pig farms. For the most part that may be true, but that wasn't the case with Bettendorf.

Bettendorf is on the eastern edge of the state and sits right on the banks of the Mississippi River on the border with Illinois. It's also part of the Quad Cities area and therefore part of the most industrialized part of the state. The area consists of Bettendorf and Davenport on

■ (Preceding page and above) I've included this 1959 Cushman to give you an example of a bad purchase. We picked it in Texas on "American Pickers" for $3,500, and it is now worth about the same. I paid too much. This was an average restoration job back in the day.

(Below) This is my first Harley-Davidson ever, a 1964 XLCH. I paid $1,700 for it after my stepfather said, "If you really want a Harley, save your money and I'll go half on it with you." When I brought it home, my mother was worried I was going to get killed riding it. My stepfather backed me up and I got to keep the bike! (Opposite page) A closeup of the paint job on the tank of the XLCH. The XLCH is now worth about $5,000.

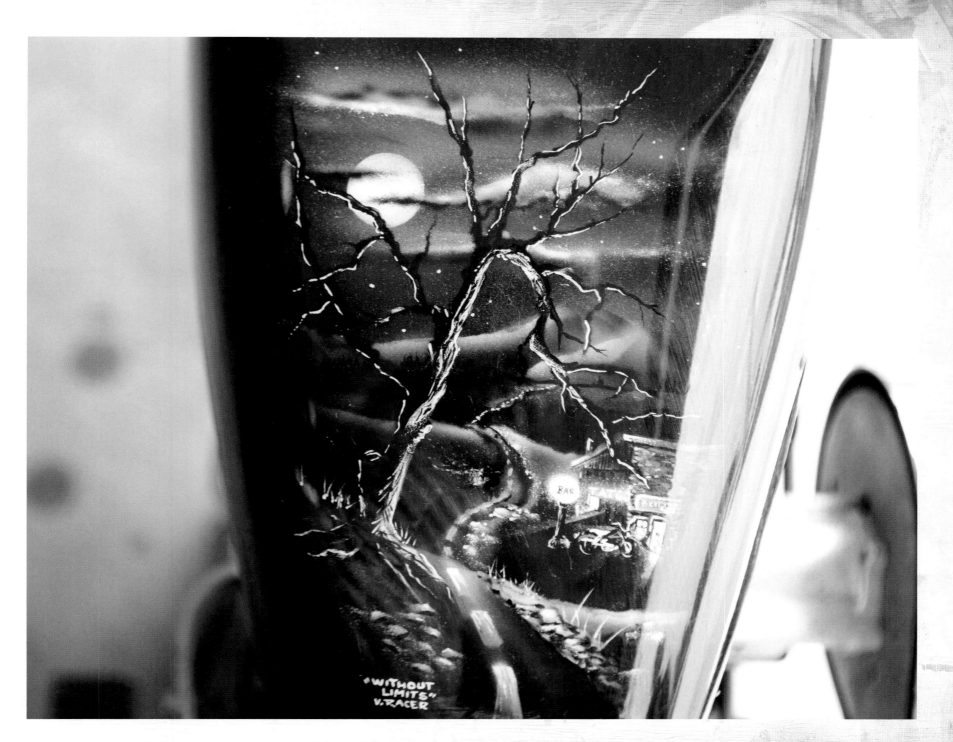

"WITHOUT LIMITS"
V. RACER

the Iowa side of the river, and the cities of Moline, East Moline and Rock Island on the Illinois side. I know that adds up to five towns, but they tried "Quint Cities" for a while and that didn't take hold, so it's still the Quad Cities.

When I was a kid, the area was booming. There was, and still is, a big Alcoa plant outside Bettendorf, and across the river were the John Deere plant, Caterpillar and International Harvester, to mention a few of the big ones. Throw in the businesses that feed off the big ones, and there were plenty of jobs for a kid back in the time.

When I got out of high school, I quit at the sprinkler company and went to work for a fire-prevention company where eventually I became a fire inspector, checking extinguishers and all the other fire-safety measures. That involved going into a lot of old warehouses and other buildings, and that's when I really got into picking. I would go into an old warehouse, and there would be some old stuff lying around in a

■ (Preceding page) To help pay for the H-D XLCH while in high school, I worked at a sprinkler company and at a hardware store. So kids out there, if you really want to buy something, consider getting a job instead of asking your parents to pay for it.

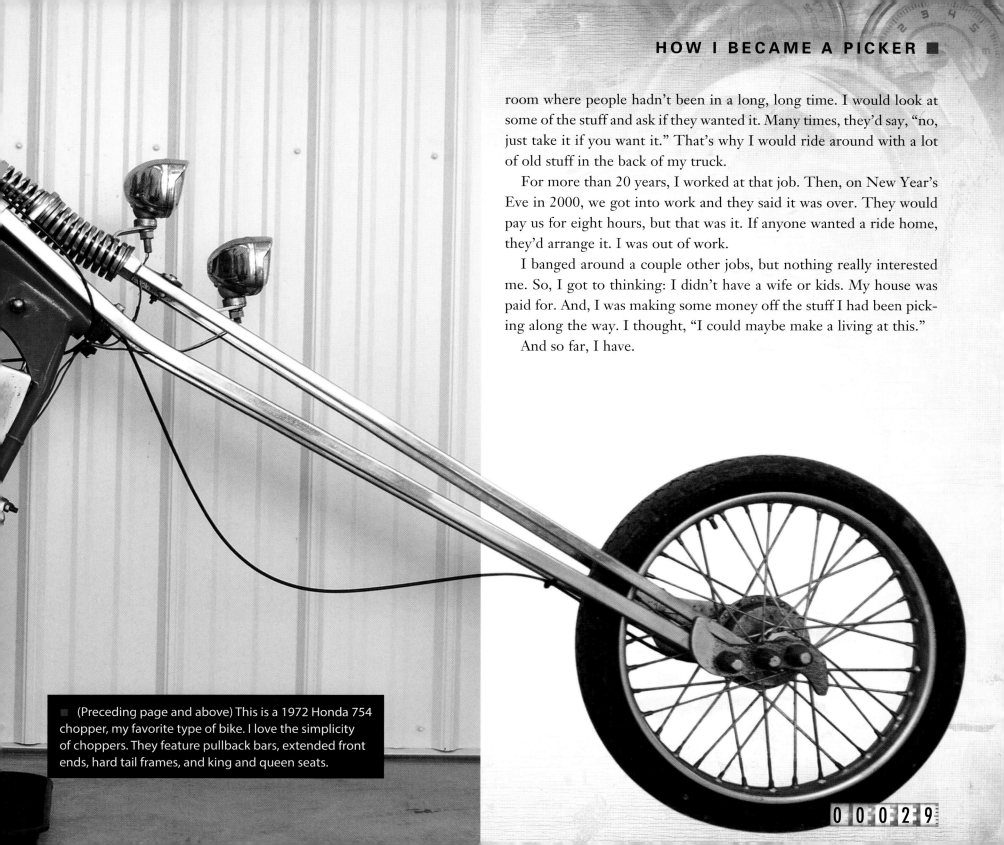

room where people hadn't been in a long, long time. I would look at some of the stuff and ask if they wanted it. Many times, they'd say, "no, just take it if you want it." That's why I would ride around with a lot of old stuff in the back of my truck.

For more than 20 years, I worked at that job. Then, on New Year's Eve in 2000, we got into work and they said it was over. They would pay us for eight hours, but that was it. If anyone wanted a ride home, they'd arrange it. I was out of work.

I banged around a couple other jobs, but nothing really interested me. So, I got to thinking: I didn't have a wife or kids. My house was paid for. And, I was making some money off the stuff I had been picking along the way. I thought, "I could maybe make a living at this."

And so far, I have.

■ (Preceding page and above) This is a 1972 Honda 754 chopper, my favorite type of bike. I love the simplicity of choppers. They feature pullback bars, extended front ends, hard tail frames, and king and queen seats.

■ (Below) After being very popular in the 1960s, choppers faded from the limelight, but then they had a little comeback about 10 years ago. (Opposite page) A closeup of the motor on the Honda 754.

■ (Preceding page) Is there any doubt who owns this 1944-45 Harley? My friend, Dave Ordt, who has been on the show, made this air cleaner for me and poked "Frank American Picker" into it! (Below) Some vintage stuff on display at the National Motorcycle Museum in Iowa.

Everyone Loves Harleys

GET ASKED A LOT ABOUT WHAT BRAND OF MOTORCY-CLE I LIKE THE BEST. THE ANSWER IS, THERE ISN'T ONE SINGLE KIND. I LIKE THEM ALL. IN FACT, I CAN'T THINK OF ANY BIKE I DON'T LIKE, EVEN THOUGH THERE IS A LOT OF JUNK OUT THERE.

THERE IS ONE TYPE OF BIKE I WOULD LOVE TO HAVE, BUT I REALLY CAN'T. THAT WOULD BE A DUAL-PURPOSE MOTORCYCLE, WITH THE BEST ONES MADE BY YAMAHA, SUZUKI AND KAWASAKI. THOSE ARE THE TYPES THAT CAN BE RIDDEN ANYWHERE, ON THE STREET OR ON THE DIRT. YOU REALLY CAN'T RIDE A DIRT BIKE VERY WELL ON THE STREET, OR A STREET BIKE ON THE DIRT, BUT WITH THESE DUAL-PURPOSE MOTORCYCLES, YOU CAN DO BOTH. MY PROBLEM WITH RIDING THEM IS I'M ONLY 5-FOOT-5 — AND MY FEET CAN'T REACH THE GROUND. THAT ISN'T A PROBLEM ONCE YOU GET GOING, BUT IT IS WHEN YOU'RE STOPPING OR STARTING.

So that leaves dirt bikes and street bikes, and I really don't care what brand it is.

The most famous make, of course, is the Harley-Davidson, the maker of the first street bikes I ever owned. It's the most recognized motorcycle in the world, and its logo — that orange and black "Harley Davidson Motor Company" — is one of the 100 most-recognized brands on the planet, period.

The company was founded in Milwaukee in 1903 by William Harley and Arthur Davidson, two boyhood friends who were then in their early 20s. The first Harley-Davidson, however, didn't go all that well. It was built, as was the norm at the time, on a bicycle frame with a small engine. The problem was, it wasn't powerful enough to climb any of the hills around Milwaukee, and that town on Lake Michigan isn't exactly mountainous.

It was back to the drawing board, and this time they got it right. Eventually, the two youngsters were joined by two other Davidson brothers, William and Walter. Interestingly, the boys got some help with their engines from another Milwaukee rising entrepreneur, Ole Evinrude, who would go on to fame as a maker of outboard boat motors.

At the time, motorcycle racing was very popular both overseas and in the United States, and a Harley was the first to break the 100 mph barrier. There was a rush to build bikes everywhere. It is estimated that during that time, there were more than 200 manufacturers of motorcycles in the U.S., but only two would survive the Great Depression: Harley-Davidson and Indian.

What sent the company to the top, though, was war. In World War I, the military ordered 15,000 Harleys. In World War II, more than 90,000 Harleys went off to the fight. Collectors should be aware, by the way, that although H-D bikes were manufactured for four years during WWII, they all bear the same 1942 marking.

In the years following WWII, Harley-Davidson slipped past Indian as the best-selling bike in the United States, a spot Indian had held since the 1920s when the company had the two of the most popular motorcycles ever — the Indian Scout and the Indian Chief. Some of those Indians can still be found today and are very collectible, though you may have to look very hard.

Indian actually predated the Harleys. It was founded in 1901, but fell on hard times a half-century later and went bankrupt in 1953. Since then, there have been many who have tried to revive the name, but none was really successful. The latest Indians are being made now in Sioux City, Iowa, by the Polaris Company, which specializes mostly in ATVs and snowmobiles.

Harley-Davidson had some financial problems of its own in the 1970s. In 1969, AMF bought the company, and what followed over the next dozen years brought the company to the brink of bankruptcy. A flirtation with the lightweight bike market didn't help, either. That may explain why Harleys today are mostly heavyweights, 700cc or more. Eventually, a group of investors, including one of the Davidson heirs, purchased the company back from AMF, and the ship began to right itself.

Another thing happened to H-D in the late 1940s to boost the name, but the company wasn't exactly thrilled by it. That was the time of the rise of biker gangs, like in the movie "The Wild One" — the notorious and sometimes feared Hell's Angels and the Outlaws. Neither did much for Harley's image, as the gangs were mostly made up of young veterans returning from the war, still restless and rebellious. They could scare the wits out of just about everyone who happened upon them.

Today, that image is pretty much a thing of the past. We call them the "One-percenters" because that's about how much of the bikers in the country they represent.

The extent of the impact Harley-Davidson has made on bikers can be found just about everywhere. The logo is all over the place. How many people have you ever seen with a Yamaha tattoo? None probably, but there are a lot of folks out there with Harley tattoos!

And then there is Harley gear, from leathers to T-shirts, which amounts to nearly 40 percent of the Harley-Davidson sales every year. It's amazing. I can walk into a place, and there will be 50 guys in there wearing Harley stuff. Out in the parking lot, the only bike will be mine. I have a lot of stuff from Harley, but I don't wear it that much. I guess that's the reason why.

I do have a soft spot for Harleys, of course, going back to that '64, my first street bike, and which I still have today. In the meantime, I love them all, no matter the make or model.

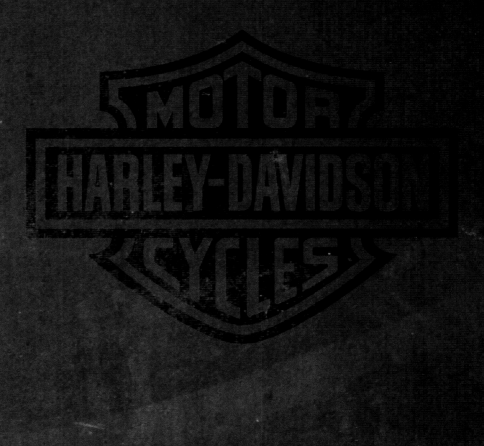

(Below) I bought this 1972 Custom Harley-Davidson Sportster on the Internet.

Tips On How to Pick Motorcycles

I've always been a collector, I guess, from the time as a little kid when I picked up rocks wherever I could find them, and pop bottles I would find along the railroad tracks and then sell.

Some of the things I've had over the years may seem a bit strange to some people.

■ (Preceding page and above) I bid on the H-D Sportster on eBay Motors, and next thing I knew, I was the rightful owner.

■ (Above and opposite page) I picked up the H-D Sportster in Charleston, South Carolina, and was pleasantly surprised that it was in better condition than I expected!

I once had a barber shop set up in my house — the old barber's chair, the straps for sharpening razors, the pole, everything. I also had a bunch of old razor-blade displays, those big pop-up displays they had in drug stores. Eventually, I moved it out, but I had it set up for quite a while.

I also had maybe 1,000 fire extinguishers I had picked up over the years during my job as a fire inspector. I still have quite a few of them.

But my main passion is collecting motorcycles. Like I said earlier, I don't how or why, but motorcycles are just in my blood.

I can't really remember the first motorcycle I collected. I just know I've bought and sold a lot of them over the years, beginning with those motorbikes that were just a frame with a lawn-mower motor on them. As I got older, I sort of graduated to dirt bikes — a Yamaha IT 175 and an RM 125, to name a couple — and then street bikes, and as I got a lot older, I'm still buying and selling motorcycles.

Over the years, I've probably bought and sold at least 400 bikes. Maybe I should have kept a log of all of them, but it's been at least that many. I still have 50 or 60 laying around my barn, including that first bike I bought, the '64 Harley. I haven't taken the time to figure out how much they're worth. They go all the way from a 1934 Harley to the 2000s. They all run, too, even that '34 Harley!

At first, I got a lot of them from George Bennett, the motorcycle mechanic instructor who lived down the street.

George also taught me a very valuable lesson: if you sold something, it had better run.

■ (Preceding page) This is a 1955 Harley Hummer that I chased down for over 20 years until the owner finally let me buy it. Everything about this bike is original: the paint, taillight, muffler, everything. It is now valued at about $4,500. (Right) A magazine ad for a H-D 125.

■ (Preceding page and above) The H-D Hummer was a 125cc bike built for fun. The true "Hummer" was manufactured in Milwaukee from 1955 to 1959.

I remember as a kid when George would put together a bike, probably a dirt bike that he had in his backyard. He would fix it and getting it running like brand new. Then, he'd take it apart again, with the parts laying all over yard.

I would holler at him, "No, no, it was running like it was."

George would just look at me and say, "OK, then let's see you put it back together and get it running." It wasn't long before I learned.

That's why, to this day, if you buy a bike from Frank Fritz, you can be sure it runs. That isn't always the case when you buy a bike from someone you don't know. Believe me, it happens all the time.

I'll go into an old barn or garage or something, and I'll ask the seller if the bike runs. He'll say, "Well, it was running when I put it in there."

Well, heck, he probably put it in there 20 years ago and didn't drain the gas tank or the oil. Nothing will run if it has been sitting for that long in that condition.

■ (Preceding page and below) This is a 1953 Harley-Davidson Panhead we bought for $7,000 on "American Pickers." It has an old motor but contains newer components, like the frame. It is now valued at about $7,500.

■ (Preceding page and above) This is my 1971 Honda 750 chopper. These were very popular in the '70s.

Be Careful What You Buy

That is the case with a lot of motorcycles you find — many of them have been put away for a very long time. Maybe it was one of their kids who had a bike and just left it when he moved on. Or maybe they kept it around because they got too old to ride anymore, and it reminded them of their youth. You have to be careful with what you buy.

I remember a few times, I'd go to look at a bike that would be in pieces hanging in the rafters. Every time, I would be assured all the parts were there, which of course they weren't all of the time.

There is one other thing, and I don't know why this is, but it always seems to be the case. If you spot a motorcycle in an old garage or warehouse, it is almost always way at the back behind tons of other junk. It would take a half-dozen strong young men to get all that stuff out of the way to get to the bike, which may not be worth looking at in the first place.

Fortunately, on the "American Pickers" we have a whole crew of strong young men who can move the stuff for us.

One of the worst buys I ever made was a Harley that was for sale for $2,100. I guess I was just too much taken by the chrome and the price. Anyway, the motor cases had been welded over and over and over again, but I was stuck with it. I worked on it for a long time, and eventually I got it to run and got my money back. But the point is to give everything a good, long look. Don't just look at the chrome.

Another thing you should know is that it's getting harder and harder to get a good price on an old bike. There are a lot more people riding these days, and a lot of them think their bikes are worth more than they really are. Once upon a time, you could ride around the countryside, spot a bike and get it at a good price. That is becoming more difficult to do now.

■ (Preceding page) I paid $2,000 for the Honda 750 chopper, plus I drove 900 miles round trip to Michigan to pick it up in the middle of winter. But it was worth it! The bike is now worth about $3,500.

■ (Below and opposite page) We bought this Kawasaki 650 custom on "American Pickers" in El Dorado, Kansas, from a guy named "Hollywood." He said it used to be in a museum. The bike is now valued at about $6,500.

00055

(Below and opposite page) I love having the Kawasaki 650 custom in my collection. It's one of my favorites as far as metric choppers go.

00056

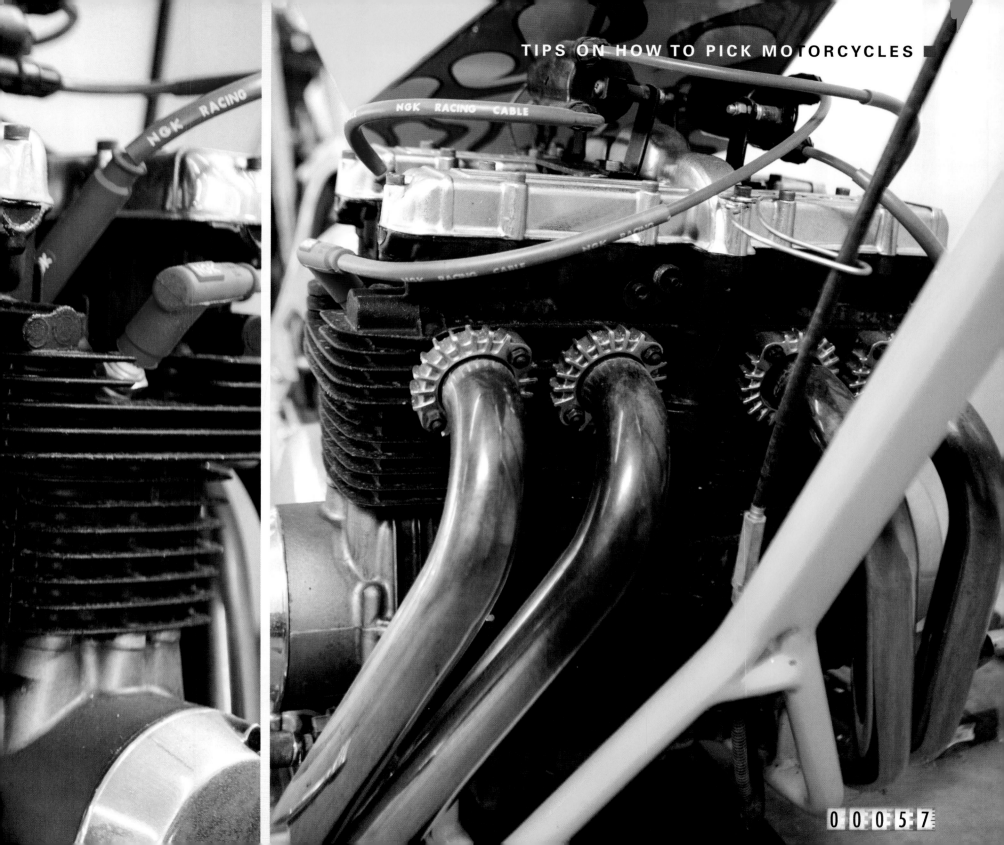

■ (Below and preceding page) My 1934 Harley-Davidson is 100 percent original, right down to the tires!

One good rule to follow is, if you want to find a good bike and perhaps sell it for a good price, go for a good stock bike, as original as you can find. And here is one other suggestion: Stay away from motorcycles painted white or green. That is because white bikes can be the color of a cloudy sky, and green bikes the color of the lush countryside. Car drivers sometimes just can't see you, like that older lady who rear-ended me because said she didn't see me, even though I was stopped at a red light.

Also, don't get taken up with all the chrome and the fancy custom paint jobs. A lot of the new riders like fancy paint jobs, and like to take off the original pipes and put on new chrome ones (which usually take away from the power, by the way). As a general rule, that takes away from the resale price.

There was a bike I was interested in one time, and it had a beautiful paint job featuring a wolf. I think that was the guy's name. He thought it added to the value, but it doesn't.

Good Deals At Swap Meets

Probably the best place to get a good deal on a motorcycle is at a swap meet, and probably the worst is one of those ads in a motorcycle magazine. At a swap meet, you can get face-to-face with someone and negotiate. In a magazine, that element isn't there.

That's the thing now — the prices are just too high compared to what they used to be. I don't mean just the dollar figure from something in the 1970s or '80s to now; I mean to what they are worth in dollars from any era.

I guess that's because of all the new riders these days. All over the country, more and more people are mounting their bikes and heading out for the weekend in the country. The old bikers, like me, call them "Weekend Warriors" or "Credit Card Riders," and sometimes "RUBs," which stands for "Rich Urban Bikers." They are the ones who, if they don't buy a brand-new motorcycle, will pay too much for a used one. That runs the price up on everyone else. On the plus side,

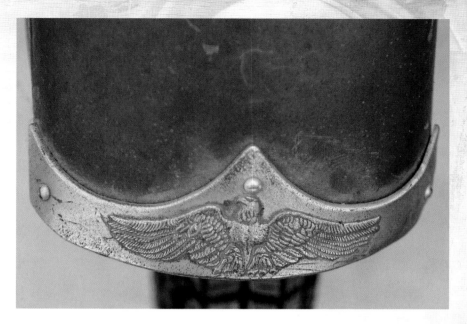

that also makes motorcycles a good investment. The values have been going up every year for a while now, with no end in sight.

Don't get me wrong, though, every once in a while, a real bargain will pop out of nowhere.

One of the best deals I ever got came in one of those most unlikely places: a Salvation Army store. A friend of mine called one day to tell me someone had donated a motorcycle to the charity, and it was for sale, and cheap. So, I hustled down there and found a 1975 BMW in great condition for $500 — at the Salvation Army, of all places!

So sometimes you can find a real bargain, and sometimes you can get a little more than you bargained for. That happened to me, too.

One day I was out riding around the countryside outside Davenport when I saw a motorcycle for sale. I went up to the house and talked to the guy about the bike — it was the one with the wolf painted on it that I mentioned earlier — but he wanted too much money.

■ (Preceding page and above) The '34 Harley is one of my favorite bikes, even with a few scratches and scrapes. I ride it all the time.

I told him no thanks, not at that price, but I went back maybe a couple weeks later and asked about it again. I wasn't ready for what I heard.

"Well then," he said, "how would you like to buy everything?"

"Everything?" I asked. "What do you mean, buy everything?"

"The house, the barn, the land, everything. All I want to take is my guns and a few other things and leave the rest."

So, we made a deal, and, instead of me paying $5,000 for a motorcycle, I had bought a house, a barn, some outbuildings and some land for $150,000. At least he threw the bike in on the deal!

I still have that place outside of town. At first, I thought I might move out there into the quiet of the country, but I found I liked the city more. Davenport may not sound like a big city, but remember that it's part of the Quad Cities, and the metro area of about a half-million people is the largest on the Mississippi River between Minneapolis-St. Paul and St. Louis.

Remember To Have Patience

One other thing you need when looking at motorcycles — or anything, for that matter — is patience. At times, the price might not be right. Or, the guy just might not want to sell.

That happened to me, and it went on for a long, long time.

Back when I was a fire inspector, I went to this business in town many times over the years, and every time I went in there, there was that pristine bike sitting in a corner. Every time, I would ask if he wanted to sell it, and he would say no. That went on for more than 20 years, until one day I drove by and saw a for-sale sign in front of the business. I went in and he told me he was retiring. Of course, I asked again about the motorcycle, and he finally said yes.

■ (Preceding page and left) I bought the '34 Harley from a farmer who had it stored in his barn for 30 or 40 years. It pays to be inquisitive –– and patient!

It was a great bike, a 1975 Harley Supersport, pure stock and in pristine condition — and I mean really, really pristine condition. It was one of the best buys I ever made. It just took a while.

We really haven't bought that many bikes on "American Pickers," probably eight at the most. But recently, my TV show partner, Mike Wolfe, and I found a beauty.

It's a 1934 Harley with a sidecar, and I was very excited. I had never owned a bike with a sidecar before and never ridden one. Oh, I rode in a sidecar before, but I never drove one and never owned one. The main reason was because they are a lot like cars when it comes to taking up space, and with all the bikes I have, I just didn't have the room for one.

But I got so excited over the '34 Harley that I didn't bother to try to get it running on my own. I hired someone to do the restoration work. It is a whole new biker experience for me, which after 40 years or so riding bikes, I guess says a lot.

While I wait for that bike to be restored, I will continue to ride what I have, which of course is quite a few motorcycles. Because of the television show, I really don't get as much time to ride as I would like, but there is still nothing quite like being out there in the country with the wind in your face.

In town, though, I do something a bit different. If I have to run some errands and it's a nice day, I'll take my Honda scooter. It's actually easier to ride, and it has more space to store things. Plus, you don't have to shift and use the clutch — just put it in gear and away you go. That may sound like heresy to some bikers, but today's scooters are not like the little buzzing things of years ago. In fact, I take my Honda out in the country and gun it to 65 miles per hour or so. The old scooters couldn't do that. That's probably why bikers don't look down as much now at the scooter riders as they once did.

■ (Opposite page) We bought this 1942 WLA Harley-Davidson bobber on "American Pickers."

HARLEY-DAVIDSON

■ (Preceding page) The '42 Harley bobber is a real period piece. It was a great find. (Below) This is a newer Triumph sport bike. I found it in a motorcycle repair shop in Nashville, and after two years of negotiating, I finally bought it for $1,500! It is fun to ride because of the new technology.

Memorable Bikes In The Movies

MOTORCYCLES AREN'T THE USUAL TRANSPOR-
TATION OF CHOICE WHEN IT COMES TO HOL-
LYWOOD. FANCY CARS? YES. TRICKED-OUT
CARS LIKE THE BATMOBILE AND JAMES BOND'S ASTON
MARTIN? OF COURSE.

BUT MOTORCYCLES? NOT VERY OFTEN.

THERE HAVE BEEN, HOWEVER, A FEW MEMORABLE
MOVIES WITH BIKES IN STARRING ROLES. THE TWO MOST
PROMINENT ARE OLD — "THE WILD ONE" FROM 1953 AND
"EASY RIDER" FROM 1969. BOTH WERE SMASH HITS AT
THE BOX OFFICE, AND BOTH SPAWNED A RASH OF COPY-
CAT FILMS, BUT MOST OF THOSE WERE DREADFULLY BAD.

"THE WILD ONE" STARRED A YOUNG, BROODING MAR-
LON BRANDO AS JOHNNY, THE LEADER OF A MOTORCY-
CLE GANG THAT TERRORIZES A SMALL TOWN IN
CALIFORNIA, ESPECIALLY AFTER THE ARRIVAL OF A RIVAL
GANG LED BY GRINGO, PLAYED BY LEE MARVIN. THE LOVE
INTEREST OF BRANDO'S CHARACTER WAS PLAYED BY
MARY MURPHY, AND THE OVERWHELMED LOCAL LAWMAN
BY ROBERT KEITH.

The motorcycle Peter Fonda rode in "Easy Rider" is on display at the National Motorcycle Museum in Anamsoa, Iowa. Originally, the bike was a Harley-Davidson Hydra Glide, but it was converted into a chopper at a shop in Los Angeles.

The bike star of the movie, ridden by Brando, was a 1950 Triumph Thunderbird 6T, something the Triumph people didn't really appreciate at first. The displeasure of the British company was one of many factors that led to the ban of the movie in Great Britain for 14 years, and when the ban was finally lifted, it still bore their "X" rating.

Ironically, when Triumph finally embraced the idea of the free publicity for its brand with Brando astride the Thunderbird, the company hired as its spokesman Gil Stratton, by then a popular American sportscaster, who played Mouse in the movie.

A raft of motorcycle B-movies followed in the late 1950s and '60s, with titles like "Hot Angel" and "Motopsycho." Much of that could be attributed to the Hell's Angels biker gang that formed in California after World War II.

It wasn't until 1969 that another decent movie featuring bikes hit the silver screen. That was "Easy Rider," a low-budget film made for less than $1 million that became the third-biggest grossing movie of the year with more than $41 million.

The movie was the brainchild of the two guys who starred in the film, Dennis Hopper and Peter Fonda, and who soon came to epitomize the "hippie" generation of the 1960s. The two wrote the script along with celebrated screenwriter Terry Southern, while Hopper was the director and Fonda the producer. It also featured the coming-out of a young actor by the name of Jack Nicholson.

The plot centers around two hippie bikers — Hopper and Fonda — who make a big drug score in Los Angeles and decide to take their booty and head to the Mardi Gras in New Orleans on their choppers. Along the way, they make some drug trips and visit a commune before taking up with an alcoholic lawyer (Nicholson). By film's end, all three meet a grisly demise at the hand of local rednecks.

The movie's motorcycle stars were four former police force Harley-Davidson Hydra Glides, circa 1948, '49 and '52, and purchased at auction for $500. All of them were transformed into classic choppers at a shop in Los Angeles. Of the four, one was destroyed at the end of the movie and the other three disappeared. One has since resurfaced in a museum in Iowa and is pictured on page 69.

There is one other memorable motorcycle scene from Hollywood, though it wasn't the focus of the film.

That would be Steve McQueen's take in "The Great Escape" after he had broken out of a German prisoner-of-war camp during World War II. The movie features a bevy of future action-movie stars, including Charles Bronson, James Garner and James Coburn. All of them escape the compound through a tunnel along with many other prisoners. All take a different path of flight — Garner in an airplane, Coburn on a bicycle and Bronson on a rowboat. McQueen's choice is to hijack a German army motorcycle.

McQueen heads toward the Switzerland border and safe refuge when he is spotted and chased by the Germans, many of whom are also on bikes. It ends when the American flier attempts to jump a double-barbed-wire fence, but becomes entangled and surrenders to the pursuing Germans. McQueen, a big-time bike enthusiast, did most of the riding in the movie, but the final jumps were not made by him, as a stuntman took over that role. McQueen's ride was — again — a Triumph, a TR-6 made over to look like a German army BMW bike.

It wasn't that motorcycles sank into that morass of bad B-movies, but they just weren't that prominent. However, when the crash-and-explode movies began to hit the big screen, bikes made a bit of comeback.

Arnold Schwarzenegger made a statement for a 1990 Harley-Davidson FLSTF Fat Boy in "Judgment Day" when he said, "I want your clothes. I want your boots. I want your motorcycle."

Then there was "The Dark Knight," the Batman movie. That bike doesn't really count, though, since it was a made-from-scratch job that even the stuntmen were wary of riding.

There were more films that drew large audiences. Ed Harris played King William in a motorized ripoff of King Arthur's Court in a "Knightriders" while astride a Honda CBX. And then there was "Mad Max," a futuristic Australian movie starring Mel Gibson and Steve Bisley, a duo described by one reviewer as the "scuzziest, yet coolest" pair of cops ever. Gibson rode a Kawasaki K-1000 and Bisley a Kawasaki 900. It spawned three sequels.

There were a couple more movies that featured bikes, but they were more on the "artistic" side rather than "action" mode. One was "The Motorcycle Diaries," an account of the renowned revolutionary Che Guevara's ride through South America as a young man. The bikes used by Guevara and his traveling buddy were Norton International cycles.

And then there was the critically acclaimed movie "The World's Fastest Indian," which had nothing to do with Native Americans, but rather a 1920 Indian Scout motorcycle. The bike was ridden by a 68-year-old New Zealander named Burt Munro, played by Sir Anthony Hopkins. Munro set land speed records on that old bike that stand to this day. The movie was excellent, and its message clear: speed doesn't necessarily kill, it exhilarates!

The Harley-Davidson XR-750 is a dirt track bike made famous by racers such as Mark Brelsford, Cal Rayborn and Jay Springsteen. This XR-750 is on display at the National Motorcycle Museum in Anamsoa, Iowa, as are the other motorcycles pictured in this chapter.

Getting Your Money's Worth

Later in this book I talk about my toy motorcycle collection, but there are a lot of folks out there who collect big toys — antique bikes and newer, tricked-up ones. They will drag them all over the country on trailers, which is why we call them "Trailer Queens." That's all they are to those guys: a big expensive toy or a piece of furniture they put in the office and then bring out every once in a while.

■ This NSU Sportmax from the 1950s is one of the coolest bikes ever made!

I really have no desire for any of them. I'm more of a common guy. I prefer bikes you can ride, not put away in a corner of your man cave. I want 'em to run, and that's why my motto could be, "ride it, don't hide it."

They are cool to look at, but I really don't want a vintage bike that doesn't run. I mean, I have some older bikes myself like a 1934 Harley with a sidecar that I just found and bought. The difference is, they run, and I can take them out on the streets — without a trailer!

■ The Triumph Thunderbird is a classic, but Triumphs in general have poor resale value.

1952

TRIUMPH THUNDERBIRD

LIKE THE ONE MARLON BRANDO RODE IN THE 1953 FILM "THE WILD ONE"

BRANDO RODE A 1950 TRIUMPH IN THE FILM. THIS BIKE IS AN GREAT EXAMPLE OF THE BIKE

ON LOAN TO THE MUSEUM

RANDY BAXTER, BAXTER CYCLE

MARNE, IOWA

My "American Pickers" partner, Mike Wolfe, buys a lot of older bikes. I think he has a couple that go back to 1910. But he collects them to sell them. I just don't want to put that much money into an old bike that doesn't run.

I must admit, though, that some of those real old collectible bikes can be pretty cool. They also can be very expensive.

There was a website a couple of years ago that came up with the 10 most expensive bikes on the market. At No. 10 was a real toy, the Bat-

If you find an old Yale like this one, buy it, because it's a true collector's item.

cycle from the 1966 "Batman" movie based on the television show starring Adam West as Batman and Burt Ward as Robin. The Batcycle was more of a movie prop than a real bike, using a motorcycle frame that was covered in fiberglass with a little sidecar for Robin. The asking price was more than $59,000.

On the other end of the list was a bike that is truly a rarity and highly prized, a 1915 Cyclone, made by the Joerns Motor Manufacturing Co. in St. Paul, Minnesota. Only 300 were ever built, and only eight are known to have survived over the last century. That bike goes for more than a half-million bucks.

■ This Harley belonged to Jay Springsteen, winner of three consecutive AMA Grand National Championships from 1976 through 1978.

That was the record until the past year when a 1954 AJS Stevens Porcupine went up for auction at the Pebble Beach Concoeurs d'elegance. That bike went for a cool $759,000. Again, the reason was rarity; only four of them were ever made.

That's a lot of money for a motorcycle, and something I would never think of. I'll go as much as $5,000 for a bike, maybe even a little more than that, but that is the absolute limit. There are a lot of bikes out there in that price range.

■ This 1948 Indian Chief was repainted yellow, unlike most that are in Indian's traditional red.

The Cyclone, like a couple of the other most expensive bikes, was a board racer. The 1915 Indian with its traditional red paint job is another board racer that brings big money on the antique market. That's the thing with the board racers; there weren't a lot of them made in the first place, so there aren't many around now.

Boardwalk racing was part of an interesting period in the evolvement of racing in this country and abroad. As the fascination with the gas-powered engine grew, so did the fascination with speed, both in cars and motorcycles. That, in turn, brought in racetracks, and with them, the board tracks.

While many people collect vintage Harleys, the most expensive bikes were made by Crocker, BMW and Vincent.

Norton International Road Racers dominated the tracks in the 1930s.

If you are a fan of racing bikes, a visit to the National Motorcycle Museum needs to be on your bucket list.

A vintage Harley with a saddlebag.

When you think of board tracks, the most obvious are the velodromes that are in arenas and are mostly used for bicycle racing. That isn't what these were. These were huge tracks paved with wood, of all things. The reason was because it was a lot cheaper to lay down planks of wood rather than pavement. And that was a lot of lumber. The biggest tracks ran anywhere from a mile and a quarter to two miles. That's about the same as the stock-car racing tracks of today. Imagine a stock-car track being paved with wood!

■ This 1971 Norton Commando Roadster was built in Britain but was popular around the world amongst collectors.

Motorcycle racing was particularly popular in the 1910s and '20s. Thousands would come out to see the daredevils roar around the track. In fact, it was estimated that around 1915, a motorcycle race in Chicago drew more people than the Indianapolis 500, which was contested over a brick track.

Speeds hit well over 100 mph even then, and you had to be totally crazy to get on one of those things. The reason was the board racers had no clutch, no throttle and, most of all, no brakes. There was only one speed, and that was flat-out, and the only way to slow it down was to hit a kill switch and wait until it came to a stop. Or you could crash, which unfortunately, a lot them did.

Many of the crashes were because of the bikes themselves. They were basically just a bicycle frame with a big motor attached, and they spewed a lot of oil as they went around the track. That, of course, made

00084

the track very slippery, and often the bikes would careen off the track and into the stands — hurting and even killing a lot of fans and riders. That's another reason they are so scarce today: production of them was pretty much shot down in the late teens after a few years of manufacture.

∎ (Preceding page, counterclockwise) A vintage Indian, Jefferson and Harley-Davidson. (Above) Older motorcycles almost looked more like bicycles!

The Great Depression in 1929 doomed most of those tracks and, with it, the popularity of motorcycle racing. It didn't do away with the bikes, though. That is why some of those older bikes are so prized today.

Most of the hot vintage motorcycles don't come from the big-name brands like Harley-Davidson. One of hottest — and most expensive — is a 1940 Crocker. The Crocker was a custom-made motorcycle and was very expensive for its time before the war. As a result, only 60 or

■ (Below and opposite page) The earliest motorcycles were board racers. Tracks were made out of wooden boards as America's fascination with speed grew in the early 1900s.

so are thought to have been made. They were huge bikes and carried a 1000cc engine. A few of them even had a 1500cc motor.

■ (Above) This 1972 Harley-Davidson belonged to daredevil Evel Knievel.

One mainstream brand that made that list of most expensive motorcycles was a 1924 BMW. It is highly valued because that was the first time the company used the emblem with which we are familiar today.

There is one other semi-mainstream brand that draws a lot of collectors, the Vincent. The British company was in business from 1928

■ This 1955 Harley-Davidson FLH is in mint condition.

to 1955, and made two of the most iconic bikes ever: the Black Shadow in 1948 and the Black Lightning in '52. Once again the draw is scarcity. The Vincents were popular, especially overseas, in the 1930s. But during World War II, the company switched to making engines for other things, such as landing boats. After the war, the company went

■ (Below) If you ever find a Harley like this in a barn or at a garage sale, call me so I can buy it!

■ (Above) A 1931 Indian Sport Scout and (below) a two-tone 1936 Harley.

1913
Harley Davidson
V-Twin 8hp, 61ci
This bike is 95% original!
In 1913 Harley produced around
18 per cent of the American built
Motorcycles with production of
12,904 motorcycles.
The first Harley V-Twin with all
chain drivers was introduced also in
1913.
Graciously on loan to the National
Motorcycle Museum

■ (Above) A classic 1913 Harley, although it could use a paint job.
(Opposite page) One neat thing about the National Motorcycle
Museum is that the bikes are displayed by brand, such as all the
Harleys in one area so you can see the evolution that took place.

back to motorcycles, but with money tight, demand went down and only 11,000 or so were made until the company went out of business.

The brand still lives on, though. In one of the most famous motorcycle pictures ever, champion racer Rollie Free, spread-eagle on a Black Lightning and wearing only a Speedo, set a land speed record on the Bonneville Salt Flats in Utah in 1948. If you can find one, you can have it for a couple hundred thousand bucks.

Foreign makes are popular right now, too. A bike like the Ducati, one of the world's best track bikes, is a draw for the collecting crowd. I don't like them, though. For one thing, they are very difficult to

1967 HARLEY-DAVIDSON SPRINT 250 SS

An Italian-American Hybrid that filled the gap in Harley's line.

In the 1960s and '70s, U.S. manufacturer Harley-Davidson imported some Italian Aermacchi bikes and sold them under the Harley name. The first to be imported in 1961 was the Sprint. This light and agile little bike was popular in Italy and used for daily transportation. However, compared to U.S. bikes it was a lightweight and didn't prove durable enough for most users. In addition, while the 250cc engine was considered a serious engine in Italy, it wasn't in the United States, where many kids' motorcycles had engines that size. Sprints can still be found today and are popular in clubs like the American Historic Racing Motorcycle Association (AHRMA).

Production and Design
Produced by Aermacchi in Italy and imported by Harley-Davidson between the years of 1961 and 1968, the Sprint was a small, compact and lightweight bike that maneuvered well and was quite agile. It weighed in at only 271 pounds.

Speed
Harley-Davidson claimed the Sprint's power was 21 hp at 7,250 rpm. According to Motorcycle Classics, "Cycle World" tested the Sprint H in 1962, which produced a 0-to-60-mph time of 15 seconds, and a quarter-mile time of 19.2 seconds, with a top speed of 76 mph.

Engine
The engine for the Sprint was a 250cc horizontal four-stroke. This proved to be too small for U.S. users and was eventually replaced by a 350cc engine on the SS model. The Sprint averaged between 45 and 55 miles per gallon, explaining why it was a popular commuter motorcycle in Italy.

Price
Retail price for a 1967 Sprint, according to Motorcycle Classics, was $750; a cherry Sprint will run between $1,800 to $4,000 as of October 2010. Many Sprints, however, require partial to full restoration because of their age.

PICKED BY AMERICAN PICKERS

NATIONAL MOTORCYCLE MUSEUM — ANAMOSA, IOWA

ON LOAN TO THE NATIONAL MOTORCYCLE MUSEUM FROM FRANK FRITZ, DAVENPORT, IA

I'm on loan to the Museum

1942
Harley Davidson
WLD

■ (Preceding page) We found this 1967 Harley Sprint while filming an episode for "American Pickers," so I donated it to the National Motorcycle Museum in Anamsoa, Iowa. (Above) Harleys, like this 1942 DeLuxe, are probably the most reliable bikes on the marketplace.

■ (Below) While this Triumph chopper looks incredibly cool, they are uncomfortable to ride over long distances. (Opposite page) The 1973 Triumph Hurricane is one Triumph that does have very good resale value. In May 2011, an X-75 Hurricane sold for $24,000 at Mecum's Original Spring Classic Auction.

maintain. If you let them sit for a couple days, the brakes lock up, and other things like that. So, they don't have a lot of resale value, at least in the U.S. They really look good, though, with that classic Italian design.

It's probably best to stay away from some of those bikes. For example, another very popular motorcycle, the Triumph, doesn't resell well either, and I really don't know why. Harleys may not be the best motorcycles on the market, but they are the most reliable, at least in the marketplace, even though some people may be tiring of them.

You can find some older bikes that will hold their value and even increase over the years. Some of the best are the Harleys from the 1950s and '60s. You can still ride them, and there are a lot of people

out there who want to buy them. Anything older than that may be cool and look good in the man cave, but they are hard to ride.

That brings up another type of motorcycle: the chopper. They were very popular in the '60s and made even more so by movies like "Easy Rider." But they faded from the scene pretty quickly, though there was a little comeback maybe 10 years ago. They're hard to ride, they're

uncomfortable and you can't carry anything on them unless you wear a backpack. Still, go to Sturgis in the summer and you'll see 25,000 of them — but they sure didn't ride them there.

There is one thing that bothers me about going out and collecting an older bike as an investment: I'm not sure about the younger riders. Maybe it's because I'm on the other side of 50 now, but I don't know

■ (Preceding page) This 1973 Magna Cycle is a work of art.
(Below) A collection of Suzukis at the National Motorcycle Museum.

about the youth of today. I'm not sure they want to mess with older bikes; they would rather just hit a button to start the bike instead of kick-starting it. Heck, they might not even know what a kick-start bike is. That's what I worry about: will there be a market 20 years from now? I really don't know, and 20 years from now, I probably won't care.

Right now, the market is pretty strong, but that goes back to my worry. A lot of today's bikers are older, and they appreciate the older bikes. Twenty years from now, their bikes will be hanging in the garage or behind that pile of other stuff with no one to buy them.

The other types of Trailer Queens are the newer bikes with all the chrome and pipes and high-end paint jobs. They can look great, but once again, they have no value to me because the owners don't ride them. Those guys would have a coronary if one of their bikes ever got a scratch on it!

Here is the major problem with those kinds of bikes, whether they are show bikes or street bikes: You go in and pay $17,000 for a new bike and then another 10 grand or so to personalize it. Just as soon as you drive it out of the lot, however, all you have is a $15,000 motorcycle, if that much. It's like that old bike I had with the paint job of a wolf looking over a lake and howling at the moon — it's fine if your name is Wolf, but not if it's Smith.

Some of these show bikers have another problem. When you are going to personalize a little older bike, be careful what kind you want to restore and spend a lot of money tricking it up. It's the same as with a car. You could take a '68 Corvette or maybe a '65 Mustang, fix it, paint it and do all of the little tricks with it, and you have something. You can't do the same thing with a Chevette or a Pinto. It's the same with motorcycles; it has to be quality to begin with.

But those folks will take whatever they have around the country to all the shows, win a little trophy and drag them home. At least they have to show that the bike will run. But all they do is kick-start it on the stage to prove it will fire up and that's it. Back on the trailer they go, back to the man cave.

It's something I just don't understand. Ride it, don't hide it!

There's Nothing Like Sturgis

THERE ARE MOTORCYCLE RALLIES, SWAP MEETS AND SIMILAR EVENTS EVERYWHERE IN THE COUNTRY THESE DAYS. AND THEN THERE IS THE STURGIS MOTORCYCLE RALLY EVERY SUMMER.

THIS AUGUST, I HEADED FOR STURGIS, SOUTH DAKOTA, FOR THE 33RD CONSECUTIVE YEAR. I STARTED AS A TEENAGER AND HAVE BEEN GOING EVERY YEAR SINCE THEN. I HOPE TO BE THERE FOR THE 75TH ANNIVERSARY IN A COUPLE YEARS, AND WITH A LITTLE LUCK, MAYBE I'LL MAKE IT FOR THE CENTENNIAL.

THE TRIP IS ALWAYS GREAT, AND THIS YEAR'S WAS ONE OF THE BEST. FIVE OF US MET IN STURGIS FOR THE WEEK AND HAD A BLAST. THAT'S NOT ALWAYS THE CASE, OF COURSE. JUST ONE GUY CAN REALLY RUIN IT FOR EVERYONE ELSE. THAT DIDN'T HAPPEN THIS TIME, HOWEVER.

00103

That really is the beauty of the whole experience. People from all walks of life from all over the country come here for a week and just have a good time. Back home in Kansas or wherever, they might be lawyers or accountants or something else. But here, for a week, they're bikers. That explains why they will look — and act — like they never would back home. That goes for the women, too.

Depending on who is counting, Sturgis is the biggest event of its kind in the country, maybe in the world. The Daytona Bike Week is on the same level, with each claiming around 500,000 participants a year. But, I'll take Sturgis.

Consider this: Daytona Beach, of course, is in Florida with all its attractions and the entire Eastern seaboard to draw from. Sturgis, meanwhile, is in western South Dakota, not far from the Montana border. Sturgis has a population of just over 6,600, while Daytona has a metro area of almost a half million. South Dakota, by comparison, has a population of just over 800,000 in the entire state.

But those are just numbers. Sturgis is unique, and there is nothing else like it.

It began about the same time as Daytona, in 1938, the brain-child of a biker named Clarence "Pappy" Hoel, who had founded a club of riders called the "Jackpine Gypsies." It started as a weekend of races around a one-half-mile track — there were nine riders in the first race — and stunts by the rid-

ers. There are still races, but the crash events of earlier years are a thing of the past. A hill climb and motocross have been added. It has grown every year since, with exception of a year or two off during World War II.

It's not the old biker image of the rally, either. As more and more people take to their bikes everywhere in the country, more and more families are coming to Sturgis. It's really something — 500,000 or so people scattered around a small town, camping out on the semi-arid land.

They get to Sturgis in a lot of different ways. Some fly in and have their bikes shipped to the event. Some arrive in motorhomes and campers. Some haul their bikes in trailers or in the back of a pickup truck. But, to this day, the majority of them ride the whole desolate way to western South Dakota in the shadow of the famed Black Hills. I've done it all of those ways over the years.

Needless to say, it's a boon to the local economy. Some estimates put the take as $800 million for the week, which is a lot of money for a small town of just 6,627, according to the last census. A couple weeks in the summer can make it for the whole year for a lot of folks in the town.

The event has been the topic of several documentaries and television features. It even attracted a reality TV crew to follow the antics of one of the town's biggest attractions, The Full Throttle Saloon, which bills itself as the world's largest biker bar. But calling it a saloon is a bit misleading. The complex covers 30 acres, has many cabins, several stages, restaurants, stores selling everything Sturgis and, of course, a saloon. It is estimated 15,000 people a day come through doors during the 10-day event. That also means a lot of beer for a lot of thirsty bikers. It is said that every day in the wee hours of the morning, two 18-wheelers pull in to replenish the supplies.

It may be my favorite stop because the owner, Michael Ballard, is a good friend of mine. Maybe that's because we both have TV shows that follow us around. The difference is, he only has a couple of weeks to document; me and my "American Pickers" partner, Mike Wolfe, have 365 days a year.

Another good friend there is Jesse James Ellis, the lead singer of the band Jackyl, which usually plays at the Full Throttle every summer. That points up one of the major reasons to head to Sturgis — the entertainment is nonstop and includes some of the biggest names in rock and country music.

The Full Throttle might be my first place to visit, but it's not the only one in the area, nor is it the biggest, believe it or not — except for the bar, as Michael Ballard would be quick to point out.

The biggest is Buffalo Chip, which sprawls over some 800 acres just outside town. It has bars, music stages, little cabins, campsites, RV parking, showers and the like. It even has a little lake complete with a beach, called "Bikini Beach" — though I think it's pronounced "Bike-kini Beach."

Another place, which covers more than 600 acres, is the Broken Spoke. It offers about the same amenities as the other two but differs in that it is part of a chain, for lack of a better term. There is a sister operation in Daytona, which rocks the same way during Bike Week down there.

But that isn't the attraction. The big thing is the camaraderie, the stories, the parties and the bikes, which is what it's all about in the first place!

Some folks can't afford to collect vintage motorcycles, so they buy toy motorcycles instead. Pictured here are "civilian" motorcycle toys. Civilian toys are highly collectible because most toy motorcycles feature a policeman as the rider, while these feature a civilian.

Toy Motorcycle Alternative

About the only two things I buy brand new without thinking much about it are canned goods and under-wear. Everything else takes a while.

For example, I'll go out to buy a pair of work boots, and I'll ago-nize for 45 minutes to an hour. Should I buy the $89 pair or the $109 pair? What style? What kind of laces? It takes me a while to decide.

■ (Preceding page and above) These cast-iron toys were made in the 1920s. These are original toys that say "Harley-Davidson" on the sides.

But show me a toy motorcycle, and I make up mind in an instant. It's been that way for many years. Now, it has gotten to the point where I have more than 9,000 of them in my collection. They're everywhere, and all I do is look at them!

I may have 75 of the same kind, but I don't sell them. In fact, they're the only things I have that aren't for sale. I sort of look at them as my retirement plan, I guess.

Just like I did with real motorcycles, I started collecting toy motorcycles as a little kid. Whenever I saw one, I'd buy it. That's why I have so many today — they add up over the years.

I'd buy them wherever they could be found: at swap meets, garage sales, meeting other collectors, whatever. That was a part of it. It was fun buying and bartering for those toys.

But then, along came a little thing called the Internet, and it changed everything. Now, I can buy a toy bike from anywhere at any time. It takes some of the fun out of it, but it's a lot easier.

But, I have to be careful. There was a time a while back when I was guilty of BUI — Buying Under the Influence. It seems I got into the Crown Royal a bit too much, and the next thing I knew, I had spent $3,700 buying toys on the Internet.

That was a lot of toys, and I would never spend that much on a single toy motorcycle, though you can easily do that. I guess the most

■ (Preceding page) The orange toy in the middle is a unique one to find! The green one next to it is a cop wearing a silver badge and police hat. (Below) In this picture we are focusing on a Hubley 7-inch, swivel-head, cast-iron Harley-Davidson toy that was made in the 1930s. They were introduced to the public in 1981 and distributed through Harley-Davidson dealerships, where they sold for $199. They now command a price between $600 and $800.

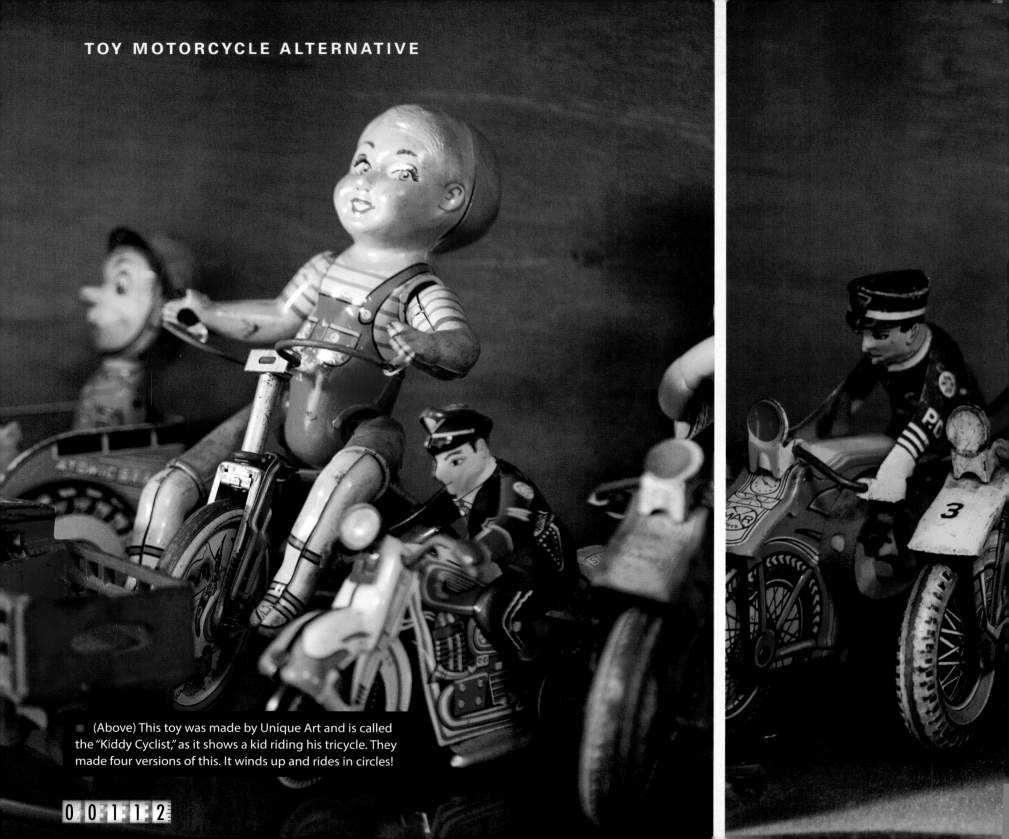

(Above) This toy was made by Unique Art and is called the "Kiddy Cyclist," as it shows a kid riding his tricycle. They made four versions of this. It winds up and rides in circles!

■ (Below) The banker-guy toy is called a "Tammy," which is a popular mechanical bank. A mechanical bank is made of cast iron and moves around to make a penny disappear. I also bought the "Old Jalopy" because it's so detailed.

■ TOY MOTORCYCLE ALTERNATIVE

I've spent on a single toy was $1,799, maybe $2,000, but they can run a lot more than that.

The most valuable toy motorcycles are the Japanese and other foreign ones. They're made of tin for the most part, and are more colorful than the cast-iron toys made here in the United States. I have a lot of both kinds, of course, but really my favorites are the cast-iron ones. They're sturdier, and just look more like the real thing to me than the tin ones.

Toy collecting has become more and more popular these days, and some can be quite valuable. If you want value, though, stay away from the big toy manufacturers, like Tonka. Those manufacturers make the toys by the thousands, so you're not going to find anything very rare. And they're not worth much unless you have the original box it came in. Even then, the box is probably going to be worth more than the toy itself.

The best-selling toy motorcycle of those mass-produced ones was by Ideal and featured one of the most iconic and unusual characters in American pop culture: Evel Knievel.

I was just a kid when he was in his heyday, the late 1960s and '70s. Just as I got into bikes at that time, Evel was one of the hottest things going. In fact, there has been no one who rode a motorcycle who was more famous than he was. Everyone knew who Evel Knievel was.

For the people younger than my 50 years, Evel may need a reintroduction. He was a stunt motorcycle rider who jumped his bikes over just about anything — a box of rattlesnakes with a couple of mountain

■ (Below) This is a 4 1/2-inch "crash car" in my collection. (Opposite page) These are Japanese lithograph motorcycle toys. They are some of the most collectable toys ever made because of the bright colors and great detail. The one in the upper right is battery operated, while the one on the bottom right is a wind-up toy. The two on the left are friction-operated toys.

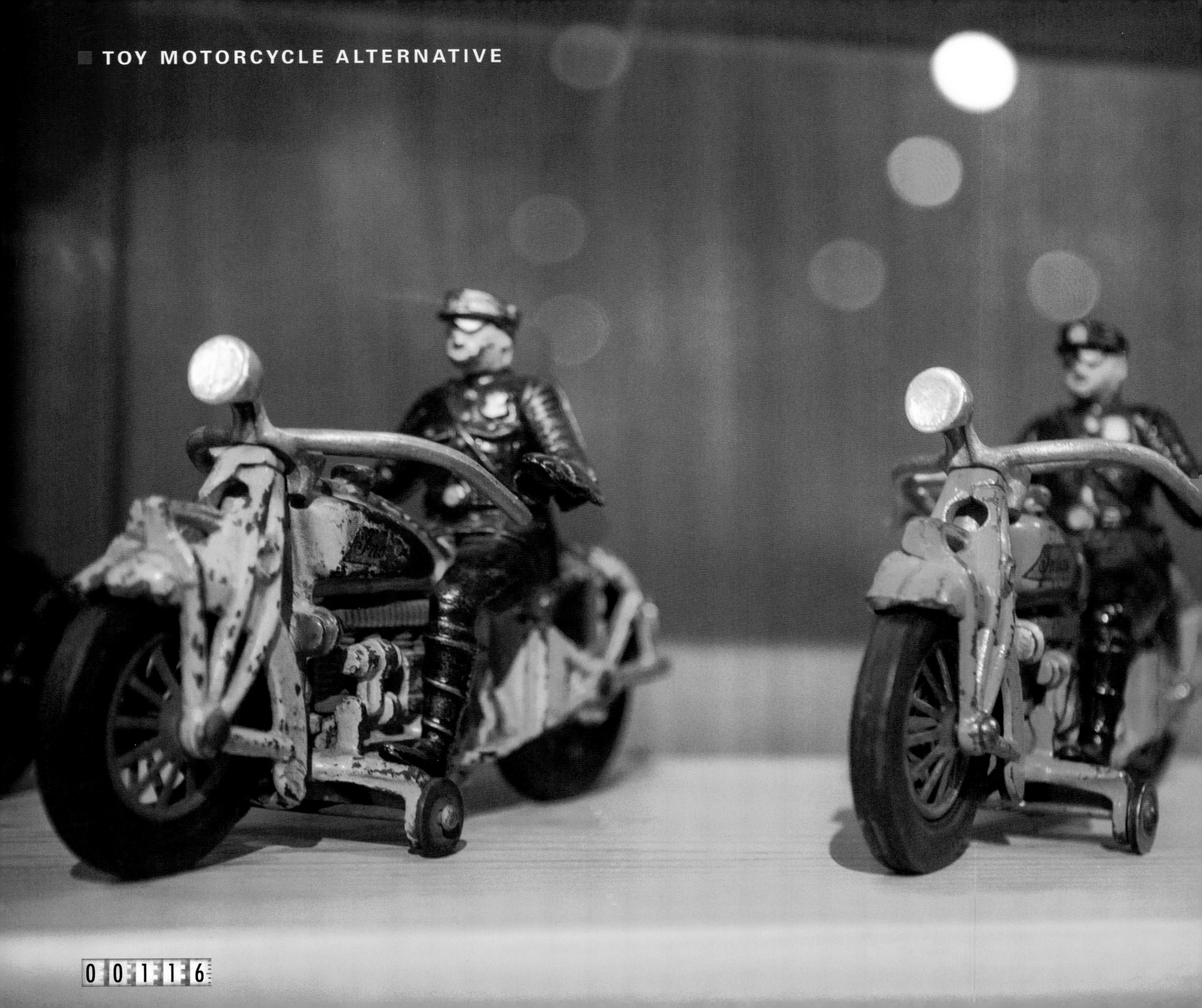

lions thrown in for good measure, rows of cars or trucks or buses, or even a tank full of sharks. It was a daredevil act that captivated a lot of the country at the time.

The strange thing is, he is most remembered for his failures rather than his successes. His first big jump was over the fountain at Caesar's Palace in Las Vegas, but he crashed and spent 20 days in a coma. He tried to jump 19 buses in Wembley Stadium in London, England, before 90,000 paying customers, but he crashed. However, he did make the record books. Over his career, he reportedly broke 453 bones, which was recorded in the *Guinness World Records* book as the most ever by a human — a living human anyway.

His most famous failure, however, was an aborted jump over the Snake River Canyon in Idaho. This was long before the days of reality television, of course, and this was reality TV at its best. It wasn't on regular TV, but on pay-per-view, and a lot of people paid to see him try the stunt. They didn't get much for their money.

Knievel was on a bike dubbed the "Skycycle," which really wasn't a bike at all. It was a steam-powered contraption that actually was registered in the state of Idaho as an airplane rather than a motorcycle.

■ (Preceding page and above) These are Hubley toy motorcycles called "Indian Fours." These are very expensive, ranging from $3,000 to $5,000 each.

Of course, he crashed. The so-called bike went down right after launch, and Evel rode a parachute into the river. He didn't drown, but he could have.

Anyway, Ideal capitalized on this, and came out with a line of toys featuring the daredevil. The company estimates it made more than 1.5 million of the toys. They were almost like Barbie dolls, and even included his son Robbie — who followed in his dad's footsteps — matched to a female character, Derry Daredevil.

Knievel rode several different bikes over his career — from a Honda to a Norton to a Lacarda to a Triumph to the motorcycle he is most associated with, a Harley XR750. He and Harley had a bit of a falling out at one time, but he got back into the company's good graces.

There is an exhibit of Knievel in the Harley-Davidson museum in Milwaukee with a life-size figure of the rider, his XR750 and a replica of the Skycycle.

A lot of the older toy motorcycles many times feature a policeman on a bike, but it could be anything from Popeye the sailor to Batman.

I have more than a few of all of them, I guess. But, they're not for sale.

■ (Above) This is another beautiful, highly detailed Japanese friction toy. (Opposite page) These are called "Say it with Flowers." They are some of the most highly collectible cast-iron motorcycle toys around. They are very hard to find, and expensive when found.

(Above) My collection of Japanese tin toy motorcycles. Good thing I don't get too carried away with my hobby!

The Best Deals I've Made

The subject comes up a lot: What's the best deal you ever made? I've made a lot of good deals over the years, but what the question really means is, how much money did you make on the deal?

Well, when it comes to motorcycles, you can make some money, but you can't make a lot of money. A bike can be a solid investment, but you're not going to make a ton of money on one. Back in the day, maybe yes, but not anymore.

■ THE BEST DEALS I'VE MADE

The reason is that there's just too much out there nowadays. People are all over the Internet now, and a lot of them want a whole lot more money for their motorcycle than it is worth. A bike might be worth $2,500, and the guy is asking $4,000 for it. You may get him down to $3,000, but you would still get taken on the deal.

As far as I'm concerned, I'm not out to scam anybody. I don't like to go to a garage sale or something and scam a little old lady out of a bike and she has no idea what it's worth. I don't do that. I pay a fair price and sell at a fair price. It helps me sleep at night.

That's why the deals I remember the most — and I've bought and sold thousands of bikes over the years — were the ones where I felt both sides came out feeling good about it.

One of the first I remember was a Benelli 650 dirt bike with only 453 miles on it. I had sort of moved on from dirt bikes, and I really didn't want them anymore. But it had a locked-up motor on it, and nobody really wanted it in that condition.

Then one day, I ran across a Benelli collector. He was into all types of the Italian bikes, and we made a deal. I paid about $800 for the dirt bike and sold it for $1,500. Considering what I put into it, I didn't make a lot of money on it, but the collector took it and restored it. I guess you could say I found the bike a good home.

Benelli, by the way, is an interesting bike. It's Italian, and the company is the oldest motorcycle manufacturer in Europe, established in 1911 by a mother who wanted to find work for her six sons. There were a lot of them sold in the United States years ago, and that is the interesting part. The bikes were sold through the mail-order catalog company Montgomery Ward. A lot of people out in the country got their first bike through "Monkey Ward," as it was popularly known around the country in those days.

I made another collector happy with a bike I had, a '63 Honda 350 Dream. That particular year and model came in only three colors — black, red and white. There were plenty of the black ones and red ones to be found, but he couldn't find a white one anywhere until he found

■ (Above) A vintage Benelli dirt bike. (Opposite page) My 1971 Harley.

mine. I can't remember what I made on the bike, but that wasn't the point. The smile on his face made it all worthwhile. I love a deal that is good for both sides, like the white Honda I sold to the collector. If you make a really fair deal, you will feel good about it, and so will the other guy. To me, that's a memorable deal.

Another deal like that was a 1978 Kawasaki LTD1000. It hadn't run in a long time, but I cleaned it up and tuned it up and got it running again. Once again, I didn't make a lot of money on it, but it turned out to be worth more than just money.

I sold it to an older fellow who had once been a rider, but who hadn't been on a bike in a long time. He just wanted to get back in the saddle again. But, he didn't have a lot of money. I let him have the bike for probably a lot less than I could have gotten from somebody else. But that wasn't the point. This guy just wanted to get out there and ride again, get out in the country and feel the wind in his face. So I helped a guy, and that should make anyone feel good.

■ (Above) A Kawasaki LTD1000. (Opposite page) My 1964 Harley.

That isn't to say you can't make anything on a deal. Yes, you can, but it has to be the right circumstance. Or, you can move too quickly. That happened to me, too.

I bought a Ducati 450 Scrambler for about $600, and as usual, I cleaned it up and had it running smoothly. Rather than sell it like I usually did, I went to the Internet. Of course, this is the way a lot, if not most, deals get made these days.

I didn't know much about the Ducati, except that it was Italian and had the reputation as one of the finest racing bikes in the world. But, I'm not a racer. I'm a rider, so I didn't care much about that.

Anyway, I put it up for auction on eBay. When it got to $2,800, I let it go. As it turns out, the guy who bought the bike was thrilled because he said he was willing to go to $4,500 for it. So, technically, I lost some money, but I didn't feel bad about it. It was a good deal all around for everybody.

The Ducati brings up another point. A bike like that — one that is not your usual common brand — will do better on the market. Harleys are everywhere and can be had on the cheap, but the same goes for reselling. You have to sell on the cheap. The demand might be there, but so is the supply.

And speaking of buying on the cheap, the best buy I ever had was a 1978 BMW I got at the Salvation Army for $500. I felt a little bad about it since I probably should have paid a bit more. But it hadn't been ridden in 20 years or so and needed some work to get it running. I got it running eventually and sold it to another collector for $1,300.

Again, I didn't make a lot, but I had rescued a motorcycle and put it in the right guy's hands. That made me feel good.

There were a couple other bikes that made me feel good, too.

One I bought from my uncle Dave, who is the husband of my mother's sister. I didn't pay much for it, and I didn't make much when I sold it, but that wasn't the important thing. What was important was what I learned from it.

In the first place, it was a kick-start-only bike, a 1971 Harley Sportster. Not many people want a kick-start-only bike, especially the younger riders. They want a push button or a key to turn, not a kick-start. You can't blame them. A kick-start can flip a rider over the handlebars, or you can break an ankle. You have to be careful, and for most riders, it isn't worth it.

That wasn't what made that a great buy for me, though. What made it great was what I learned. Uncle Dave couldn't get it moving, but I decided to give it a shot. I worked hard on that bike, real hard. I learned a lot, and the knowledge I got I use to this day. That makes it priceless to me.

Finally, the best buy I ever made, I still have. It's that old '64 Harley Sportster, the first street bike I ever had. I had it because of my stepdad. As I told you earlier in the book, he used to let me take his Harley around the block when my mother wasn't looking. He knew how badly I wanted a street bike — I was already riding dirt bikes — but I was 14

■ (Above) The Ducati 450 Scrambler transaction was a good deal for everybody.

and couldn't buy one, nor could I ride one legally. So, he made me an offer I couldn't refuse. He would buy it and put up half the money if I would work and put up the other half.

I came up with my half of the $1,700 price, and he put in the rest, and then we went down and made the buy. I had my first bike, and I still have it!

I still ride that bike out in the country, feeling the freedom a motorcycle can give you and feeling the wind in my face.

Isn't that what it's all about anyway?